WITNEY

IN OLD PHOTOGRAPHS

WITNEY
IN OLD PHOTOGRAPHS

—— COLLECTED BY ——
TOM WORLEY

ALAN SUTTON
1987

Alan Sutton Publishing Limited
Brunswick Road · Gloucester

First published 1987

British Library Cataloguing in Publication Data

Witney in old photographhs.
1. Witney (Oxfordshire)—History—
Pictorial works   2. Witney (Oxfordshire)—
Description—Views
I. Worley, Tom
942.5′71   DA690.W83

ISBN 0-86299-439-X

Typesetting and origination by
Alan Sutton Publishing Limited.
Printed in Great Britain
by WBC Print Limited, Bristol.

CONTENTS

INTRODUCTION   7

1. STREETS AND BUILDINGS   9

2. BUSINESS AND INDUSTRY   39

3. TRANSPORT, THE MARKET AND PICTURES OF INTEREST   69

4. SCHOOLS, THE WAR AND THE MILITARY   87

5. PEOPLE AND EVENTS   113

6. ENTERTAINMENTS AND ORGANISATIONS   143

    ACKNOWLEDGEMENTS   160

INTRODUCTION

There are probably some feelings of nostalgia in all of us, and older folk sometimes remind us of the good old days. Well, what was the past really like?

Witney's history has been researched and books have been written. This book, however, deals mainly with the mid 1800s and up to c. 1946, and forms a visual record of that period. There are a few pictures from after this date, and a few pre-date the camera in the form of drawings, paintings, etc. This is necessary in order to get a glimpse of the town in the early Victorian times.

There was much more character to the buildings, and hardly two were built alike during this period, but would we want to go back to dark, cold and draughty houses?

The military is well recorded from the days of the Oxfordshire Militia. Pictures also show the volunteers (territorials) in their scarlet (pre-boer war) uniforms. Carnivals, fairs, sporting groups, school treats etc., give us a glimpse of Witney at play, and many people with roots in the town will no doubt enjoy looking at the groups to find their forefathers. Today, many products come from the dozens of different factories in the town, but Witney of yesteryear depended almost entirely on the manufacture of blankets (which were, and still are, world famous) and to a lesser degree, on glove making. While looking at this section it is interesting to see how labour intensive these firms were. Both industries were large employers of women and the working day was long. Some townsfolk will remember the many mill hooters in the morning calling the workers to their place of employment. We also note that although industrial relations were good, there were a few strikes, one of which was settled during the great war when the boss appealed to the weavers to go back as they were letting down the soldiers in France.

It is refreshing to see the streets free from motor vehicles, and everyone living at a slower pace, without the noise, pollution and danger that the internal combustion engine has brought.

The population in 1911 was 3500 and the town developed very slowly until the 1930s. Since the Second World War and particularly during the 1970s and 1980s after Witney was designated a growth town, houses have been built in large numbers, necessitating the development of a new shopping centre with a large car parking area. Fortunately this has been done tastefully, behind the main part of the town and the older buildings remain intact. It has, however, had a traumatic effect on the old established businesses and in the next few years we could see yet more changes.

Research in museums and libraries has revealed much of interest, some of which has been included in the captions. I gratefully acknowledge the assistance readily given by many people and offer my thanks at the back of the book. We have a wonderful old town with an interesting history and I have had great pleasure researching and compiling this book. I hope that readers will enjoy the fruits of my labour.

Tom Worley,
Witney, 1987.

Witney High Street c.1804. The layout of the town is clearly recognisable today from this old picture and a few of the buildings still remain. The large house in the centre distance is the Batt house which is now a school.

Streets and Buildings

The northern end of High Street. The date is unknown but it is probably c. 1850. The new link road, opened in 1987, enters on the extreme left of the picture.

High Street c. 1880 viewed from the outside the Methodist church, looking south. The tall house (extreme left) was the minister's house: it was pulled down in 1893. Today Welch Way (construction of which started in 1961) enters High Street on the right of the picture.

Mid High Street, probably in the early 1900s. What was then primarily a residential street became one of the main shopping areas.

The Middle High Street in late 1920s, when the pedal cycle was the popular means of transport.

Winter scene in the lower High Street, 25 April 1908.

A cottage in High Street. It survived until about the 1950s when it was demolished and Backs Coach company then used the site for garaging and repairs. Today it is the entrance to a small housing development.

The Congregational Church believed to have been established in Witney in 1662. This building was opened 1 October 1828. The building and grounds cost £2000. It was pulled down in 1971 and a supermarket now occupies the High Street site.

The southern end of High Street showing the coffee tavern on the right. This then became the Temperance Hotel and later the Central Cafe. Boots the chemist now occupy the site. Late 1800s.

The entrance to the High Street, looking north. The Temperance Hotel is on the right. The streets are busy with horse traffic, c.1905.

Cook & Boggis, draper, traded in Witney from c. 1898, in premises formerly occupied by Edward Lower. The business was sold in the early 1960s and in December 1964 a serious fire destroyed the building. A supermarket was built on the site and Waitrose occupied it. During 1987 the site was redeveloped as part of the new shopping centre and several businesses now trade there.

The Marlborough Hotel was a staging post where horses would be stabled and changed ready for the next stage of the journey.

Seventeenth-century Town Hall, the Butter Cross and shops in the centre block of the Market Square. The shops include Harris & Son, jeweller and clockmaker and Joseph Stoddart, draper, trade names long since forgotten, c. 1867.

Market Square c. 1924–1930. Isaac Busby, draper, occupied the central shop.

The Market Square on the right and a view down the hill in the late 1800s. Thomas Perdue, chemist, occupied the shop on the extreme right of the picture.

The Market Square c. 1900, with a passenger carriage waiting outside the Marlborough Arms coaching hotel.

The southern end of the Market Square, showing the Bull Inn which was closed in 1969 and converted into an estate agent's office. The other businesses include Saltmarsh & Druce (established 1873), The Angel Inn and Leigh & Son which are still in existence today.

The War Memorial, built in memory of the men who died in the Great War of 1914/18, was dedicated in 1919. This picture was probably taken in the early 1930s.

The Town Hall, believed to be seventeenth-century. Witney is the centre of a farming area and had a thriving market on Thursday each week. Under the arches of the Town Hall corn was bought and sold, c. 1900.

Corn Street corner 26 May 1935. The Silver Jubilee of King George V and Queen Mary. W.H. Tarrant traded on this site as a wholesale grocer.

Witney's famous landmark 'the Butter Cross' where farmers' wives would sell their dairy produce years ago. The origin of the Butter Cross is not known, but the cupola was added by William Blake of Cogges in 1683 and the illuminated clock was added in 1889 through public subscription. Late 1800.

Witney Cemetery in 1910. The land, originally a quarry, was purchased for £170 and opened for burials in January 1857. A row of cottages nearby in Corn Street was built for the quarrymen, but these were demolished many years ago. This is the site of a traffic roundabout today at the confluence of five roads.

An early engraving of the Butter Cross. Two farmers' wives sell their live poultry to two gentlemen, seen near to the left corner pillar.

An artist's impression of the Bishop of Winchester's Palace. It was situated close to St Marys Church. It disappeared many years ago. Recently, however, the foundations have been excavated and it is hoped that at some future date the site will be opened up for the public to see.

The two pictures on this page, when placed end to end, show a panorama of part of High Street and the lower end of Market Square. It is a copy of a painting by S. Jones, 1828.

Pinnacle House (on the left of the top picture) was the post office for many years. In the centre is the tall building now occupied by Boots the Chemist. On the right of the lower picture is the area which reopened as a redeveloped shopping area in 1987.

Shops on the east side of the Market Square including Mr W.T. Ransom's chemist shop. This was pulled down in 1969 to make a road into Waitrose car park. During the summer of 1987 a new shop was built in the gap. c. 1930.

Demolition of the old 'Crown Hotel' which was formerly a coaching inn. April 1981.

Steeplejacks with the weather cock from the top of St Mary's church steeple. Thought to be early 1900s.

Houses on the west side of Church Green, 1888.

Although this book is principally of photographs, it is necessary to include a few drawings and paintings to show what the town was like before the days of the camera.

Drawing of Church Green by John S. Austin dated 1856. Some of the houses are still in existence today. The fashions are interesting.

Joseph Green's drawing probably pre-dates the John Austin drawing.

A large derelict house overlooking the river Windrush. The old humpbacked bridge is just off the picture to the right. Date unknown but thought to be mid 1800s.

The Bridge, Witney

The old three-arch bridge erected in 1822 and replaced in 1926. In 1967 the new bridge had to be widened. Smith's blanket factory was extended after they pulled down the building with the tall church-type window and the adjoining cottages. Late 1800s.

A closer look at the cottages in Bridge Street and the building with the large window which was a school. Late 1800s.

This and the following three pictures show Newland before the road was widened and straightened. In fact, at this time, there was a very small amount of traffic. Mid 1920s.

This is the main London to South Wales road, before the mass-produced motor vehicles cluttered our highways. All traffic went right through the centre of Witney.

This picture, looking towards the Oxford Hill, shows Mr Dix's bakery on the left. Some years later, when the motor car clogged the town, the whole block of buildings was removed and the road straightened.

The same area, looking towards Witney. Later, as motor vehicles made life on this busy thoroughfare very difficult, a bypass around the town was built and opened in April 1977.

Old houses at the Hailey end of West End. The date is probably at some time in the early 1900s.

West End from the middle to the junction at the end of Bridge Street. Not very different from today, except that there is no motor traffic.

The lower end of Corn Street. 1905.

Middle Corn Street. Note the thatched cottage on the right.

The Market Square end of Corn Street in the 1930s.

The High Street flooded; a photograph taken on 4 July 1915. As the roads nearer to the river did not flood, it is apparent that a faulty drainage system was the cause.

Flood water entered many of the shops and this picture, taken in the 1940s, shows the problems faced by the shopkeepers. The shop-fronts of most of these buildings have now been modernised and many have changed ownership.

William Seely was an architect in the town and it is through his eyes and his skill with a pencil that we know quite a lot about the town before the camera was invented.

The Corn Returns Office, drawn in 1849 by William Seely. It was replaced in 1863 by the Corn Exchange.

The corner of Corn Street in 1887 before the two corner buildings were demolished. J. Rose's shop on the left was replaced by the building now occupied by Leigh & Son. A large grocery warehouse replaced the Lamb Inn.

The old four-arch bridge which was replaced in 1822.

HOUSE IN BRIDGE STREET.

The humpback bridge on the right and cottages in Bridge Street.

This Seely drawing entitled 'Woodgreen Common' shows Woodgreen in 1848 before Holy Trinity Church was built.

SECTION TWO

Business and Industry

R. Fenemore, butcher, with the Christmas fat stock display. The business passed to his son Harry and then to grandson Percy. 76 High Street in 1921.

International Stores, 26 High Street, c. 1908. A chemist now occupies the site.

Before the days of factory mass production and supermarket distribution there were many small family bakers. This one was at 86 High Street. The building was pulled down in 1986 to make way for the new link road which opened in 1987. The photograph was taken in 1936.

Sam Carter ran the Central Cafe in the 1930s and Mrs Brown had the teashop next door, on the left of the picture. Boots the chemist now occupy the two sites.

G. Harris, newsagent and hairdresser, 15 Bridge Street. The boy on the left later emigrated to Australia, returning with the army to fight in the Great War when, alas, he was killed.

22 Market Square (next to the Midland Bank). Mr Shepherd at his shop door and Mr William Hitchman, a barber who lived nearby.

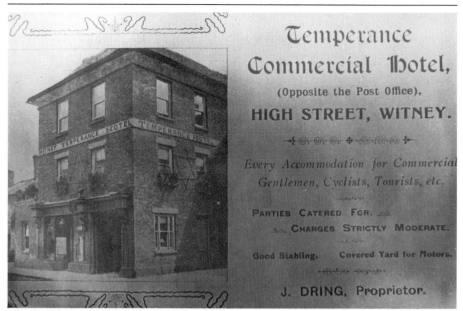

Temperance Commercial Hotel,

(Opposite the Post Office),

HIGH STREET, WITNEY.

Every Accommodation for Commercial Gentlemen, Cyclists, Tourists, etc.

PARTIES CATERED FOR. CHARGES STRICTLY MODERATE.

Good Stabling.   Covered Yard for Motors.

J. DRING, Proprietor.

The Temperance Hotel was formerly the Coffee Tavern. At the southern end of the High Street.

There were many carriage makers in the 1890s as this was the age of horse transport. E.T. Hadden was at 85 High Street.

MRS. WALTER HARRIS

WHOLESALE and RETAIL

FRUITERER & CONFECTIONER

HIGH STREET, WITNEY.

(Next to Post Office.)

MRS. W. H. begs to inform her numerous customers that she has one of the largest and choicest stock of

SUGAR TOYS

In all the newest designs suitable for the CHRISTMAS SEASON, from ¼d. to 6d. each, also a choice stock of Fancy Figures, Boxes and Baskets full of the Best Chocolates and Sweets from 1d. to 6d. each. Xmas Stockings full of Sweets and Toys from ½d. to 3d. each. Bonbons 1d, 6d, and 9d. per box. Splendid Mixed Sweets at 3d. and 4d. per lb. Oranges splendid value from 12 to 40 a Shilling. Lemons from 12 to 16 a Shilling. Almeira Grapes 8d. per lb. Kent Cob Nuts 7d. per lb. New Brazil Nuts 1896 crop, 5d. per lb. New Almond Nuts, Chestnuts, Black Spanish and all other kinds of Nuts of the best quality at the lowest possible prices. ates very choice 2d., 3d., and 4d. per lb. Finest Bosnian Plums 5d. and 6d. per lb. Figs, new season, 3d., 4d., and 6d. per lb.

This advertisement appeared in the Witney Gazette on 19 December 1896. No other comment is needed, except a reminder that a farthing was equal to 0.104p, the 6d equivalent to 2½p and 40 oranges for a shilling is the equivalent of 8 for 1p.

Mr Fitze tailor's shop after a fire (April 1909). Mr Huddleston purchased the site and built the 'People's Palace' cinema.

The Witney Blanket Company was started here at 39 Market Square (now Lloyds Bank) in 1913. It became a large national mail-order company after moving to a new factory on the Leys in 1921.

Witney Cinema in the 1920s. It gave a final performance and closed in January 1985.

W.H. Tarrant's grocery shop, 32 Market Square. It was burnt out on 11 June 1911; the coronation day of King George V. It was later rebuilt.

Dean's cash stores (a small general grocers) was at the northern end of High Street.

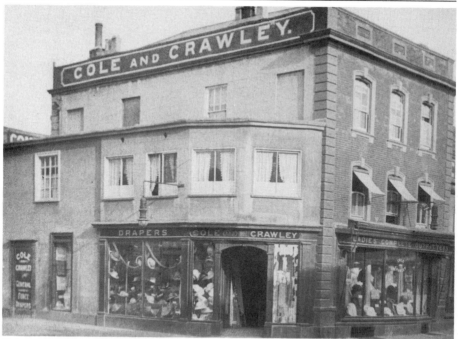

Cole and Crawley occupied this prominent site in Market Square from c. 1912–1918. They were complete ladies outfitters. When they left, Izaac Busby took over the business.

Shops in the High Street decorated with bunting for the coronation of King George V, 11 June 1911. The shop painted white was Mr List's butchers shop, now the central fruit shop. On the right, Eatons shoe shop is now owned by Farmers.

This small sweet shop and general store was at Staple Hall, a part of the Court Inn.

This grocery business, situated in the middle of Corn Street, passed from father to son through three generations. They were also specialist bacon curers, supplying home cured hams and all the by-products, such as lard, brawn, etc.

23 High Street c.1910. W. Witcher, hairdresser. This property, in the middle of High Street, was demolished c. 1963. The National Westminster Bank now occupies the site.

Osborn Tite was founded in 1882 and closed down in 1976. Waterloo House, as it was then called, has been converted into an arcade of small shops called Waterloo Walk. Tite's sold ladies' and gents' clothing. 1906.

E.A. Long, 108 High Street, near the bridge. He took over the business in 1895.

Henry Brooks & Co., in the middle of High Street c. 1900, Miss E. Delnevo has traded on the site since the autumn of 1958. Brooks & Co. were taken over by Dingles who moved to the Market Square.

Corn Street Stores, together with West End Stores, a shop in the Market Square and a large wholesale warehouse were all owned by W.H. Tarrant.

Samuel Leigh & Son, established in the mid 1800s, are still trading at the corner of Corn Street.

The two pictures on this page show the delivery vehicles of Messrs Leigh the Ironmonger, probably in the 1920s.

Shops on the east side of Market Square, showing the chemists shop of Mr W.T. Ransom. This shop was pulled down in 1969 to make an access for the Waitrose car park. During the summer of 1987 a similar type of shop was built to fill the gap. Mr Ransom was a photographer in his spare time and most of the pictures taken of the Square in this book are his work.

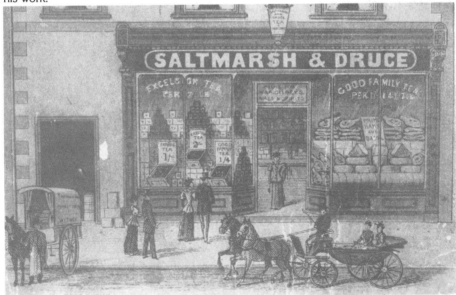

Saltmarsh and Druce, established in 1873 and still trading under the same ownership. The picture is taken from the front cover of their 1897 catalogue of prices.

KING. GEORGE VI. CORONATION. MAY. 12th 1937. GLOVE SHOP. DECORATIONS.

Witney had a thriving glove industry and this picture shows one of the workrooms of Pritchetts glove factory, on the occasion of the coronation of King George VI on 12 May 1937.

The morning after the fire which destroyed Pritchetts factory, 14 April 1926. Employees viewing the wreckage are, left to right: Dick Ayres, Alan Haley, Len Moss, Charles Pumfrey, Bill Glaister, Jim Townsend.

Leather Cutters at Pritchetts Glove Factory, c. 1924.

John Pumfrey and Elsie Pimm bring leather from drying to the glove cutters. Pritchetts Glove Factory, c.1924.

Blanket making has been the principal industry and biggest employer of labour in Witney for over 300 years. There was always a need for female labour for weaving and machining.

Hand loom weaving; an early method of blanket making before the invention of the automatic looms.

Fred Botherton operating an old hand loom. In later years the hand loom was only employed to make a special cloth used for horse collars.

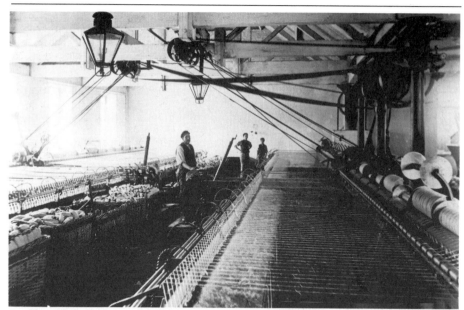

A self-acting spinning mule. This process twisted the yarn into a continuous thread and wound it on to bobbins ready for use on the looms. 1898.

In the middle of the noisy weaving shed, this girl sits winding special dyed yarn on to bobbins to be used for binding the ends of blankets. 1898.

Weavers and their looms. 1920.

Blankets hanging in a sulphur bleach house. 1898.

Tuckers (blanket finishers) carry a length of washed and bleached blanket to the racks for drying and stretching to the full correct width. 1920.

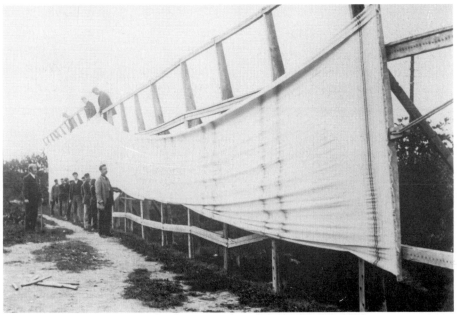

Blankets being hung on tenterhooks to stretch and dry in the sun. 1898.

The Dye House. 1898.

Various locations in and around the town were used for the many processes of blanket-making. Here, blanket lengths are being loaded onto a horse-drawn dray for transportation to the warehouse for the finishing process. 1898.

Carding. Hand raising after leaving the nap-raising machine. Each piece of blanket is examined in a strong light to check for faults and gone over with a hand card.

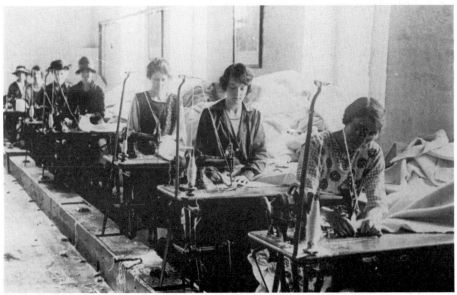
Whipping (oversewing) the cut ends of the blankets to prevent fraying. 1920.

A group of tuckers pose in front of blankets which have been hung on the racks. 1898.

Weavers and Gig Shop employees. Mr Harry Broome was the foreman (centre back row) in the early 1900s.

A new boiler *en route* for Early's Witney Mills in 1896. It was installed by Daniel Young; a firm of engineers in Bridge Street which was founded in 1872.

The Great Western Railway draymen with bales of blankets, collected from the factories for despatch from the goods station at Witney to all parts of the world.

Mill girls on strike at Witney Mills, before 1918. Employees of the Bliss Tweed mill at Chipping Norton came over and joined the picket.

Early's factory in Mill Street after a fire in January 1905.

The two views on this page, when joined end to end, form one picture of Smith's Crawley Mills. Blankets are drying on racks in the background, while other blankets are spread out in the fields to catch the dew. This greatly assisted the next process of carding (raising the nap).

This factory is no longer connected with the blanket industry. It is now a small industrial complex with diverse businesses.

Marriott's Mill employees on strike because of a reduction of wages. There were a few mob riots and the strike lasted a week. One girl was sacked for allegedly laughing at the boss. May 1908.

A weaver at her top swing loom in one of the blanket factories, 1940.

Transport, the Market and Pictures of Interest

The 3.35 p.m. passenger train from Oxford. It would pass through Witney on its way to the end of the line at Fairford. It was affectionately known locally as the *Fairford Flyer*. 1960.

Mr W. Eaton, station master, with the office staff in bowler hats and the porters in uniform. Mr W. Payne, (second from the left, back row) was the taxi man who met the trains with his horse and wagon, c. 1890.

The number of station staff suggests that Witney was a very busy station. The picture is believed to have been taken c. 1900. The last passenger service was in 1962. The station is now lost under an industrial estate.

John Simpson, a GWR driver, collects bales of blankets from Early's factory, c. 1940.

A complete train load of blankets at the goods station in Witney in 1911. 1970 saw the end of the railway in Witney, when the Beeching 'axe' closed the branch line from Yarnton.

Witney's passenger station – a photograph taken shortly after the 1939/45 war.

Bible Class outing to the British Empire Exhibition at Wembley. There were 190 people in the party. About eight bus loads stretched a long way down the middle of High Street on 21 June 1924. Note the solid tyres and folding hood for wet weather.

The Three Pigeons pub outing to Wales. As they found the Welsh pubs closed they returned via Gloucester. The driver was John Wilsdon (on the left). 1930s.

The Robin Hood pub outing was a day out for all the family, c. 1936.

Harry Haines, chauffeur to Mr Bernard Smith – a blanket mill owner. At one time he was chauffeur to General Smuts. Harry Haines later became an industrialist with quarries and a fleet of lorries.

Mr Sam Leigh out for a spin in his new sporty model.

Charles Foster takes churns of milk from Mr Paxton's farm at Hardwick to the railway station for despatch by train. 1908.

Mr Beckinsale, Manor Farm, Curbridge, delivers milk in Witney. Note the price: 6*d* per quart (2 pints for 2½p) delivered to your door.

Sidney Hart delivers bread in Witney for Mr Lord, baker, 16 Corn Street. He took over the business when Mr Lord retired. The photograph was taken in the 1930s.

G.W. Townsend; fried fish delivery by bicycle. The date is not known but it could be 1930s.

Joe Monk poses on his primitive motorized bicycle.

Two seats in front and one at the rear behind the driver. It appears to have been a most uncomfortable ride on this three-wheeler.

This ox-drawn covered wagon, advertising 'Atora Beef Suet', passed through Witney in the 1930s.

August 1930 and a surprise for the Witney folk as the airship R100 passes overhead on a return flight from Canada.

A BE2a military plane which crash-landed in a field at New Leys on the Curbridge Road in 1913.

Witney's fires were attended by this horse-drawn hand-operated pump. The date was 1889. The firemen were: (on the engine), Harry Broome, –?– , (standing), Hedley Vickers, John Rose.

The Fire Brigade c. 1900. Back row: Hadden, Collier, Bob Warner, H. Shuffrey. Second row: Harris, Fennemore. Third row: Graham, Long, F.M. Green (capt), W. Payne, J. Rose, H. Vickers. Front row, seated: Middleton, Harry Broome.

Firemen showing their newly-acquired Leyland Tiger Engine, 1937. On the engine: Joe Jones, Fred Jones, John Johnson, Bert Jones, A.E. Taphouse, Philip Eaton. In front: Jack Burton, Jack Barnes, Jack Busby, Ronald Keates, O. Valentine (captain), Jack Prior, Harold Turner, Jim Jones.

Thursday, market day, c. 1900.

The Sheep Market. Pens were quickly erected by tying hurdles together. 1906.

Farmers take up their positions, awaiting the auction of the sheep in the Market Square, c. 1930. The Market ceased to sell animals in the Square in 1963.

The Water Tower was opened in 1903 near the junction with the main Oxford to Cheltenham road. It burst in February 1904 and this picture shows repair work being carried out.

A familiar scene from the Crawley Road in the 1920s and 30s. A large stone quarry on the town's outskirts. The Quarry Road housing estate has covered all evidence of the workings.

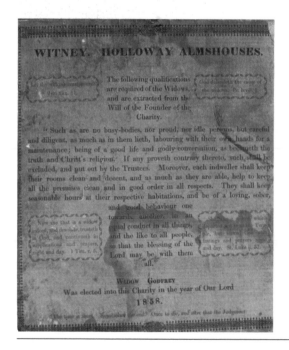

WITNEY. HOLLOWAY ALMSHOUSES.

The following qualifications are required of the Widows, and are extracted from the Will of the Founder of the Charity.

" Such as are no busy-bodies, nor proud, nor idle persons, but careful and diligent, as much as in them lieth, labouring with their own hands for a maintenance; being of a good life and godly conversation, as becometh the truth and Christ's religion.' If any proveth contrary thereto, such shall be excluded, and put out by the Trustees. Moreover, each indweller shall keep their rooms clean and decent, and as much as they are able, help to keep all the premises clean and in good order in all respects. They shall keep seasonable hours at their respective habitations, and be of a loving, sober, and good behaviour one towards another, in an equal conduct in all things, and the like to all people, so that the blessing of the Lord may be with them all.

WIDOW GODFREY
Was elected into this Charity in the year of Our Lord
1858.

A notice which hung in the Holloway Almshouses, situated adjacent to St Mary's Church, 1858.

The old Langle Bridge over the river Windrush connecting Crown Lane with Langle Common, (today Langle is often spelt Langel).

Several large houses on Church Green and in the High Street had long gardens running down to the river. This picture shows one family who kept a punt at the bottom of the garden. Cogges Priory can be seen on the left. This photograph also shows the bridge which replaced the one shown in the picture above.

M. Midwinter,

LIVERY STABLES,

19 Corn Street, WITNEY.

Licensed to Let Horses, Char-a-Bancs, Brakes,
Silent Tyred Wagonettes, Broughams,
Landaus, Cabs, Pony Traps, &c.

TERMS MODERATE.

*Special terms for Private Parties on Early
Closing Days, also for Large Parties.*

This business flourished between the mid 1800s and 1920. One of Mr Midwinter's contracts was to carry mail. He would drive to Faringdon where the two horses would be changed for fresh ones for the return journey.

Children leaving the cinema after a free performance from 10.30a.m. until 11.30a.m., by kind invitation of the Witney Electric Theatre Co. This was part of celebrations on the occasion of the coronation of King George VI, 12 May 1937.

Schools, the War and the Military

A group of children from Miss Hayter's school on Church Green in 1917.

Witney Grammar School pupils and teachers around the maypole on the school playing field, c. 1900.

The Grammar School (now the Henry Box Comprehensive) was founded in 1663 by Henry Box for 30 boy pupils. Teaching was done in the middle section, with masters' accommodation in the end wings.

The Headmaster and staff of two with about 90 pupils (boys and girls). This was the Grammar School of 1910.

The fourth form room of the Grammar School in the 1920s.

Wesleyan School Group, 1896. This mixed school was erected in 1855 and enlarged in July 1884 for 450 pupils. It was situated behind the Methodist Church in High Street. Teaching at this school ceased when Witney Secondary School (now known as Woodgreen Comprehensive School) was opened on 8 September 1953.

The teachers pose before the main entrance to the Wesleyan School, 1896.

Wesleyan School group 1890. Mr J.C. Sims is the teacher on the right. The only child's name known is Sarah Seacole.

Wesleyan School Teachers 1922. Back row: Doris Cutler, Miss Hoyle, Kitty Fisher, Hilda Cox, Alice Watts. Seated: Miss Rodder (Head of Infants), Lily Ostler, J.C. Sims (Head), Sidney Gillett, Doug Stayt (Head boy), Dora Scanes.

Boys of Lynton School. This school was situated in a large house at the top of Broad Hill, overlooking Woodgreen.

West End school children dressed for May Day with their teacher Miss Flossie Harwood in 1912. The Queen's attendant was Arthur Beale and the May Queen was Elsie Hosier.

The Blake School, Cogges, 1926. Headmaster Mr Fallows, with the boys swimming team.

St Mary's Church of England Junior School, 1932.

Miss Harwood, who was a teacher at West End School, started her own school for tiny tots in Bridge Street. She is seen here with some of the children in 1955.

Three Witney men who volunteered at the beginning of the Great War in 1914. Oswald Tarrant is on the left. Sidney Smith is on the right but the other name is unknown.

The Witney detachment of the Oxfordshire Volunteer Battalion (later incorporated into the Oxfordshire and Buckinghamshire Light Infantry) in their red tunics, away at Windsor for Summer camp in 1895.

Two Witney seventeen-year-olds, members of the Oxfordshire Yeomanry in France in 1915. A.E. (Bert) Horne (on the left) was killed in action. Joe Jones (right) went through the war until almost the end when he was severely wounded. However he survived and lived until 1980.

This is probably the earliest picture of the houses on the east side of the square, the cottage on the right was pulled down shortly afterwards. Witney Company Oxfordshire Volunteers (Territorials), in their scarlet uniforms, pre 1880.

The Witney Company of the Oxfordshire Volunteer Rifle Corps parade in their scarlet uniforms. This unit was incorporated into the Oxfordshire and Buckinghamshire Light Infantry in 1908.

Witney Volunteers parade in the Market Square, *c.* 1894. The buildings in the background (on the east side of the square) are worth a second look, especially when comparing them with the present scene.

Another view of the volunteers in 1880. Fred Clappen traded in the shop in the middle of the square until 1897, selling clothing and all types of textiles including blankets.

Witney Volunteers who joined 'B' Co. Fourth Battalion Oxon and Bucks Light Infantry at Whittle near Chelmsford. They pose in the Wesleyan School playground in August 1914.

The Volunteers shown above march to the railway station on their way to a savage war from which quite a number of them did not return. August 1914.

The Queen's Own Oxfordshire Hussars, a territorial cavalry unit, in ceremonial dress. This photograph was taken when they were away at camp. The uniforms included a blue tunic and deep purple trousers. Some of these uniforms have been saved and can be seen at the Royal Greenjackets Museum at the Slade, Oxford.

The Witney Cycle Brigade. A picture taken at the Mount, a large house near to the church. 1900–1902.

The Militia. A Volunteer Battalion of the Oxfordshire Light Infantry in 1865.

Soldiers, having been on parade, leave the market square on their way to the battle front in France, January 1916.

Troops stationed in Witney during the Great War. This picture shows the guard at Leafield Radio Station. August 1914.

Lorries of the MT section of No 346 Co. ASC, with men training before they were sent to France.

Spectators at a sports event at Marriotts Close in August 1915, organized by the MT section of 347 Co. ASC an army unit based in Witney. The local newspaper reported beautiful weather and a large gate. There were 22 sporting events.

A German LVG Bomber captured at Salonica, on display in the Market Square to help raise funds for the war effort. The target was £20,000 and they actually raised £23,600. 7 March 1918.

Men from Witney and district in the trenches at Ypres, 1915. They include: Joe Jones, George Jones, Harry Miles, Wesley Miles, Harold Price, Fred Curtis. Almost all were either killed or seriously wounded.

Witney Voluntary Training Corps in the Corn Exchange. They met for training, military drill and firing on the range. The men identified here include: Messrs Hall, Hayter, Buxton, Higgs, Habgood, Swingburn, Shuffrey, Curell, Steptoe, Dawkins, J. Knight, B. Knight, J.C. Sims, in September 1915. Mr J.F. Mason was the commandant.

No.33 Training Squadron, machines and hangars at Witney Aerodrome, 11 June 1918. The road on the left is the main Oxford to Cheltenham highway. After the Second World War the area was used as a car heater factory.

The Dedication of the war memorial on Church Green on 12 September 1920.

'B' Company, Fourth Battalion Oxon and Bucks Light infantry. The Territorials at training camp, Fort Widley, just outside Portsmouth in August 1921.

German prisoners of war at the back of the Fleece Hotel where they were billeted. 19 April 1918.

Oxfordshire Constabulary, Witney sub division, 1945.

The Auxiliary Fire Service during the 1939/45 war.

The Air Observer Corps during the 1939/45 war. Their duty was to observe, identify and report on all overflying aircraft: –?–, H. Mace, C. Clarke, H. Steptoe, W.T. Crawley, –?–, N. Phipps, –?–, –?–.

Third Battalion Oxfordshire Home Guard, Witney Platoon. Originally named the LDV (Local Defence Volunteers), they were trained to army standards and were a reserve to be sent anywhere in the defence of the country in case of invasion.

Victory in Europe celebrations, 8 & 9 May 1945. The war in Europe had lasted from 3 September 1939 and peace was a joyous occasion. Spontaneous dancing took place in the Market Square.

National Service Parade during War Weapons Week. The Home Guard on 14 September 1941.

National Service Parade during War Weapons Week. The Auxiliary Fire Service on 14
September 1941.

National Service Parade during War Weapons Week. Youth Groups including Scouts,
Guides, etc., pass through an austere Witney on 14 September 1941.

The Royal Engineers Territorial Army (Newcastle) Band. At the outbreak of war in September 1939 this unit of volunteers was sent south and for a short while were billeted in Witney.

On 14 July 1909 they buried Corporal Edward Miles of the Staffordshire Regiment at Cogges cemetery, with full military honours. The bearers in the cortége were territorials of the Oxfordshire Yeomanry Infantry. A volley of three shots was fired as a salute over the grave.

People and Events

Wedding Group. 23 August 1906.

Rallying call in the Market Square, with the town councillors and other dignitaries seated around the front of the Corn Exchange during War Weapons Week. 14 September 1941.

Here the children of West End are at a street tea party, organized to celebrate the coronation of Queen Elizabeth II, 1953.

A street party to celebrate the end of the war. Mothers hold a tea party for the children of the Curbridge Road area in July 1945.

This street party is at No. 21 Hailey Road and celebrates the end of the war. VE Day, July 1945.

Witney Silver Jubilee celebrations, held on 6 May 1935 to commemorate 25 years reign of King George V and Queen Mary. At 7 p.m., according to the official programme, the old people would be served dinner in the Corn Exchange followed by a concert at 8 p.m.

St Marys Church Choir, c. 1930.

Holy Trinity Church Choir, 1932.

Group of Methodist Church local preachers, June 1910.

Another group of local preachers of the Methodist circuit. The date is unknown but it is probably early 1900s.

This group of children belong to the Young Leaguers; a Methodist Church organization. 15 September 1909.

A Wesleyan Chapel Bazaar on 22 November 1904. The theme was '25 little Japs'.

Corn Street Primitive Methodist Chapel Choir 1914. The building is now used as a laundrette.

The churches and chapels were very active earlier this century with strong support by the young. It was a centre for fund-raising and leisure activities. This picture shows an event for raising money for the Red Cross during the Great War, 1915.

This page is included to show some of the fashions early this century. Men with high collars, straw hats were plentiful and many 'Alberts' were in evidence.

The ladies also went through a phase of 'overdressing'. Huge hats, dresses from throat to floor and full sleeves buttoned at the wrist.

A Witney family group photograph. 1902.

Children, evacuated from the London bombing, pose for last picture as they prepare to leave for their homes, 26 June 1945.

There are many familiar faces in this Womens' Institute picture. On the occasion of a party in the Corn Exchange to celebrate their 25th anniversary. 1955.

Witney Sports Motor Cycle Club Annual Dance, held in the Corn Exchange in February 1932.

Toc H Witney branch 1935. The organization was founded by Tubby Clayton in the trenches at Ypres in the Great War. The idea was to make a sanctuary for war weary soldiers to spend a few hours of comfort and sanity before returning to the trenches. In peacetime it remained to foster a continuing comradeship.

Witney Town and Rural District Councillors and prominent townsfolk at the opening of the new waterworks, at Worsham on the river Windrush on 2 October 1936.

Major James Edmondson, the Conservative Member of Parliament for the area. He had just been re-elected on 18 December 1924.

Mr J.H. Early, a Witney blanket manufacturer, electioneering on behalf of the Liberal Party in 1922. Harry Hart, Tom Salmon, Arthur Stonebridge, J. Harold Early, Percy Viner, Tom Littleton, –?–, Fred Stayt.

Queen Elizabeth the Queen Mother visited Witney, arriving by helicopter and landing on Church Green. Here doctor and Mrs Timings are being presented. She visited the Henry Box School on the occasion of its tercentenary in 1963.

Queen Elizabeth II being escorted by Patrick (left) and Richard Early, when she visited Witney Mills, 18 April 1959.

Mr H. Shuffrey and his workmen. He had a woodworking business on Woodgreen (the building is now a large block of flats). His men made the pulpit and screen for Holy Trinity Church. Mr Will Viner (front right) was later a milkman and a town councillor, c. 1915.

'The Pierrots', an entertainment group led by Mr Fred Moore (centre back row). Other members of the troupe were: Oswald Dring, Maurice Fyfield, Harry Souch, Sidney Florey, Mabel Amor, Blanche Collins, Maud Fyfield, Edith Keates, Eva Jordan, Hilda Cox and Elsie Keates. 1910.

Postmen outside the sorting office at 1 High Street in 1914. Back row: H. Hancock, F. Witcher, –?–, –?–, –?–. Middle row: C. Keates, J. Bowler, A. Busby, D. Thomas, J. Millin, –?–, J. Clarke. Front row: H. Warner, J. Hart, –?–, Miss Horne, Mrs Adams, Merriman, W. Long, H. Godfrey.

A Baby Show held in 1918 in the grounds of Woodlands, a large house overlooking Woodgreen which is now a nursing home.

Collecting for the YMCA during the Great War. Standing: Janet Early, Dorothy Bartlett, wife of Church Army man, Mrs Crosbie (wife of the minister). Seated: Church Army man, Miss Morris, –?–.

Workers' Union Demonstration at Witney. The visitor, Tom Webster, was a top line cartoonist who worked for the Daily Mail for many years.

Employees of Smiths Bridge Street Mills out on strike, c. 1920.

The St Johns Ambulance Brigade photographed in their meeting room, the Congregational Church Sunday School room, at the rear of the church in the High Street, c. 1950s.

Bridge Street Mills Band, May 1891.

Witney Town Band at Charlbury Flower Show in 1898.

Witney Town Band in the 1920s.

The band had just received their new uniforms in this 1936 photograph. George Morton (behind big drum) was the bandmaster.

With the people milling round, and I hope appreciating what they hear, the town band plays in the Market Square during the 1920s.

The Dominoes Dance Band, 6 July 1937. Cecil Bishop, Frank Wilkinson, Frank Hanford, Sidney Smith and Wally Arthurs.

The Rythmic Aces Dance Band in 1938. Arthur Clack, Douglas Lomax, Jim Bridgman, Jim Millin, Don Heynes and Stan Horne.

The Novelty Dance Orchestra in the mid 1920s. Jack Kempster, who kept a music shop, is at the piano.

Cecil Hick's Melody Makers, with Cecil on drums. Mrs Huddleston is the violinist, Alf Smith plays saxophone and Sid Lewis at the piano, early 1920s.

The Fair, known locally as Witney Feast, in September 1900. This picture shows the roundabouts on Church Green. A few years later the fair moved to the recreation ground, 'The Leys'.

Taylor's Electric Coliseum, early 1900s. The top of the bill reads 'Driven from home', 'Drink and repentance' and all for two pence entrance fee.

A good general view of the fair on the Church green in 1900. Sometimes there were too many shows for the green and the overspill would occupy the roadway, and even stretch as far as the Market Square.

A general view of Witney Feast during the 1920s on the Leys.

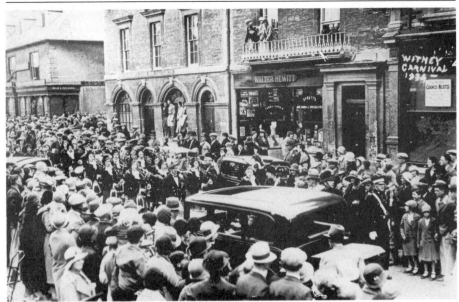

Witney Carnival was an annual event organized by the British Legion. It was started shortly after the Great War to raise funds to help ex-service men in need. This 1936 picture shows the Dagenham Girl Pipers, who were the main attraction at Marriotts Close after a procession.

This old car was an entry in the Carnival vehicles section in 1935. Judging would take place on Woodgreen before the parade through the town.

Here a parade passes through the High Street in 1929. The leading vehicle was entered by
Percy Bartlett, a grocer who became a noted sausage manufacturer.

There was a section for decorated prams and carts; some of the entries were quite ingenious. 6 June 1938.

There were many entries in individual fancy dress. Everyone was out to enjoy themselves. 1934.

A group of spectators at Marriotts Close (the football field behind the High Street) in 1930. Entertainment would be provided in the centre arena.

The most spectacular displays at the carnival were the decorated vehicles, and anyone owning a lorry or horse and dray was in great demand by the factories, youth groups etc. This is one of the 1933 entries.

SECTION SIX

Entertainments and Organisations

Procession which included the Oxfordshire Yeomanry, descending Broad Hill. It is believed that the parade was to celebrate the end of the Boer War in 1902.

A day of joyous celebrations marred only by the very wet weather. Led by the town band, this is part of the victory parade in 1919 to give thanks for the ending of the Great War.

Every year in the summer the Wesleyan School and St Marys Church of England School would hold their treat in a field in Farm Mill Lane. The children would parade through the town to the field for sports followed by tea, cakes and sweets. This parade is in High Street, c. 1905.

Children with their Union Jacks followed by the Boys Brigade band. They are taking part in celebrations on the occasion of the coronation of King George V on 11 June 1911. Here they are passing over the old Witney Bridge.

The School Parade pass over the bridge and into High Street. c. 1905.

On a fine day lots of people would turn out to see the parade of children on the day of their treat. These are children from St Marys Church of England School in 1904.

Here the parade of Sunday School children pass the old post office on their way to Marriotts field in Farm Mill Lane, quite close to St Marys Church, 1 August 1911.

Marriotts Field where the Sunday School children pose for the cameraman. 1 August 1911.

The Wesleyan School Treat Parade passes through the southern end of the High Street. June 1914.

The Witney Team that won the Oxfordshire Football Association Challenge Cup, 1894 season.

Witney Cygnets Football Club. Winners of the Witney and District League, 1908/09 season.

Members of the Witney Bowls Club in the 1920s.

Bridge Street Mills Cricket Club on Witney Mills Ground, 1905.

Old Gramarians Cricket Club. Mr Wood the school headmaster is seated in the centre of the front row, c. 1938.

Witney Bowls Club, 1955.

The Great Marathon Race, 8 October 1910, at the corner of Corn Street. Jess Scarrott, Bert Scarrott, Ern. Price, –?–, –?–, Blackie Bridgewater.

Two photographs taken during the Great War. The Baths' attendant (in a straw hat) was a refugee from Belgium. The boys are believed to be from the Lynton School.

Swimming in the river Windrush. This is where several generations of Witney folk learnt to swim. The small changing cubicles were pulled down in the 1930s and rebuilt farther back, leaving a grass sunbathing area by the river. The new indoor pool opened in 1975 making this area obsolete.

Children showing the latest fashions in swimwear in August 1915. The 'Heath Robinson' construction with steps is the diving board.

The Boys Brigade pose in front of the Wesleyan school doorway. Mr J.H. Early (behind the big drum) was the captain, c. 1912. Note some boys carry dummy rifles which were used for drill, and the stretcher in foreground was used for first aid training.

Mr J.H. Early helped to form the Boys Brigade in Witney in 1903 and was a lieutenant under Mr J.C. Sims. Shortly after he was made captain he was succeeded by Mr A.H. Rowley in the late 1930s. Mr Early's son Richard took over the company in 1947, retiring 25 years later in 1972. Thus in 69 years there were only four captains. The picture was taken on 6 May 1935.

A Boys Brigade camp at Freshwater on the Isle of Wight, c. 1910. For many boys this was the first time they had left home.

Not many people were up early enough to see the Boys Brigade leave for camp. However on their return, as this picture shows, quite a number of people were at the station to greet them. They would march back to the Methodist Hall behind their band. 1903.

Revd Unsworth on the left with the Witney scout troop in 1926. One of these boys grew up to be quite famous in the world of medicine.

Scouts and cubs line up for a photograph outside the Church House, c. 1933.

An early picture of the Guides at camp.

Guides and Brownies c. 1926. They met in a building adjacent to the Methodist Church in High Street.

Proclamation of King Edward VII, 26 January 1901. The Bailiffs were W. Brooks and J. Saltmarsh.

Proclamation of King George V, 10 May 1910, with Bailiff Mr C. Story and Council Chairman Mr E. Tarrant. There was a fanfare at 12.30 at Staple Hall and the proclamation read by the bailiff. Then a procession to Parliament House in Corn Street where it was read a second time. Finally there was a procession to the Town Hall (picture) followed by the third and last reading of the proclamation.

An Ox Roast in Corn Street. Neither the date nor the occasion is known.

An Ox Roast in the Market Square to celebrate the coronation of King Edward VII, 26 June 1902.

Machinists stitching gloves at Pritchetts Factory.

PHOTOGRAPH CREDITS

My thanks to Dr Malcolm Graham and his staff at Oxford local history library, for pictures and assistance. Also to John Willoughby, Royal Greenjackets Museum, Oxford and to: Miss P. Ranson, Mrs A. Brooks, Mr A. Bartlett-Taylor, for their particular knowledge of Witney of old.

Also thanks to the following: Mr P. Barker, Mrs J. Bartlett, Mr W. Bridgwater, Mrs E. Buckingham, Mrs P. Collicutt, Mr Ken Cook, Mr G. Cooper, Mrs M. Dingle, Mrs E. Gibbons, Mr & Mrs D. Hawker, Mr & Mrs J. Hirons, Mrs Horton, Mr A. Jewell, Mr & Mrs L. Seely, Mrs R. Seely, Mr & Mrs F.K. Wilkinson, Mrs L. Wilsdon, for pictures and information.

I would also like to say a special thank you to the people who, over many years, have lent me their photographs for copying, thus enabling a much wider view of Witney in days gone by. Finally it would be wrong to omit a mention of the many people whose original work, whether it be prints, paintings, drawings or photographs, has made this book possible.

TOM WORLEY. 1987.